POP PERFORMANCE PIECES

Alto Saxophone & Piano

Published by
Chester Music
part of Wise Music Group
14-15 Berners Street,
London W1T 3LJ, UK.

Exclusive Distributors:
Hal Leonard
7777 West Bluemound Road,
Milwaukee, WI 53213
Email: info@halleonard.com

Hal Leonard Europe Limited
42 Wigmore Street, Marylebone,
London W1U 2 RY
Email: info@halleonardeurope.com

Hal Leonard Australia Pty. Ltd.
4 Lentara Court, Cheltenham,
Victoria 9132, Australia
Email: info@halleonard.com.au

Order No. CH85063
ISBN 978-1-78558-334-6

This book © Copyright 2016 Hal Leonard

Piano scores are transposed.
Chord symbols at concert pitch.

Alto saxophone consultant: Howard McGill.
Piano consultant: Lisa Cox.
Compiled and edited by Naomi Cook.
Music formatted by Sarah Lofthouse, SEL Music Art Ltd.

Photographs courtesy of Ruth Keating, assisted by Lisa Cox and James Welland. Special thanks to the pupils at St Benedict's School, Ealing and their Director of Music Christopher Eastwood for taking part in the photo shoot.

Printed in the EU.

www.halleonard.com

CHESTER MUSIC

ALL OF ME

Words & Music by John Legend & Tobias Gad

Hints & Tips: Make sure you use the dynamics to help build interest in the piece, being careful not to overpower the melody. There are many held notes throughout — resist the urge to rely on the pedal to sustain the notes rather than holding them for their full value. Practise without the pedal first!

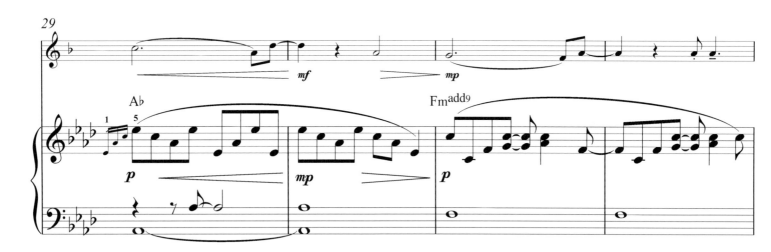

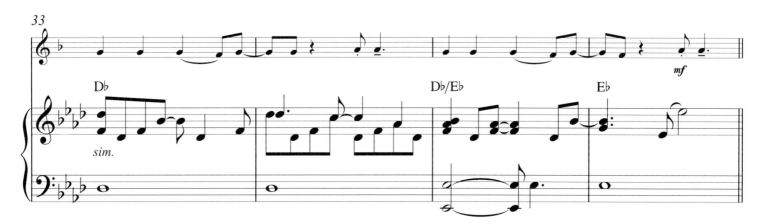

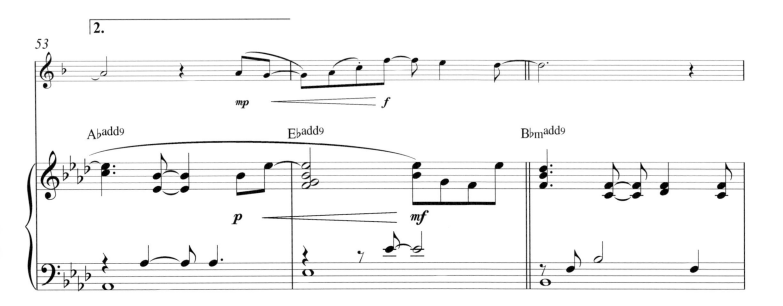

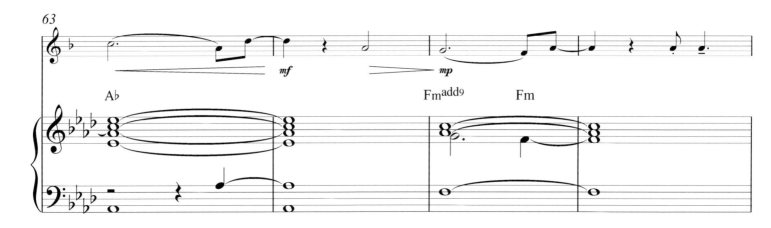

D.S. al Coda

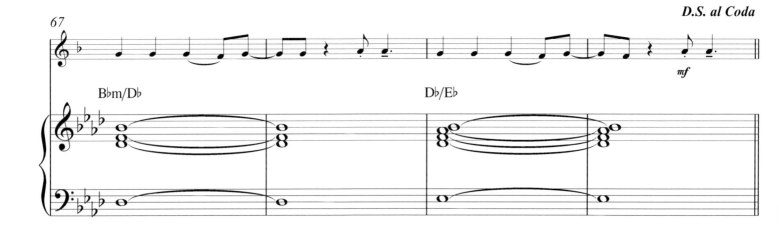

BRIDGE OVER TROUBLED WATER

Words & Music by Paul Simon

Hints & Tips: There are lots of block chords in this piece: make sure you use the correct fingers in anticipation of the next chord position. Watch out for the accidentals too!

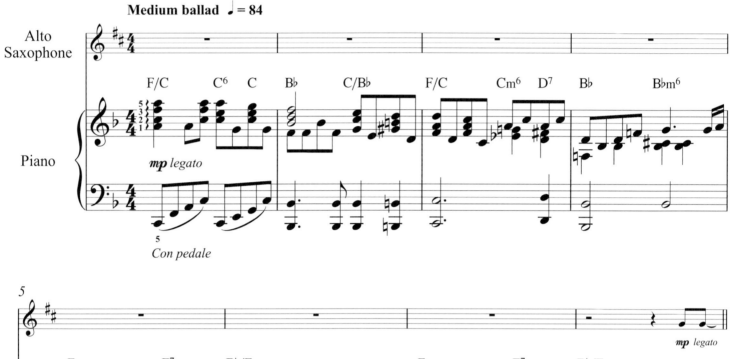

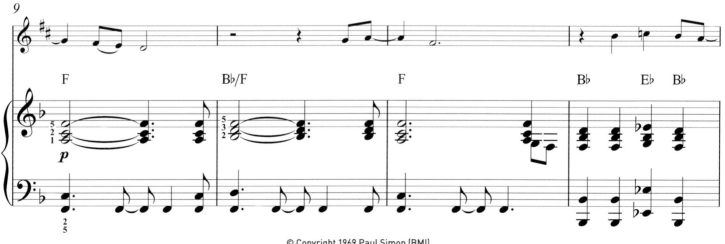

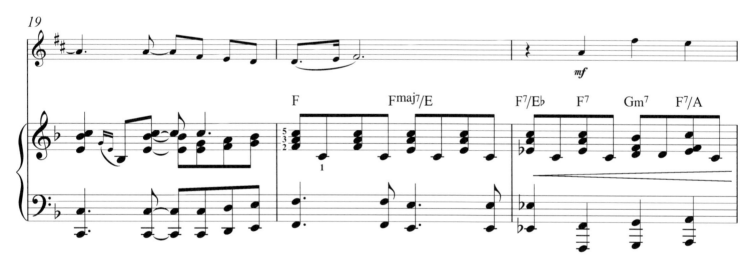

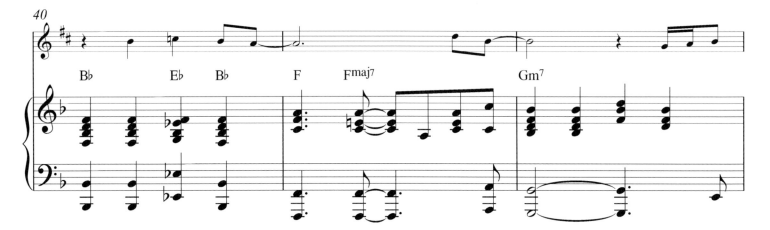

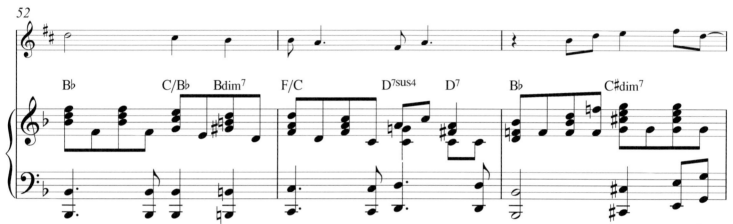

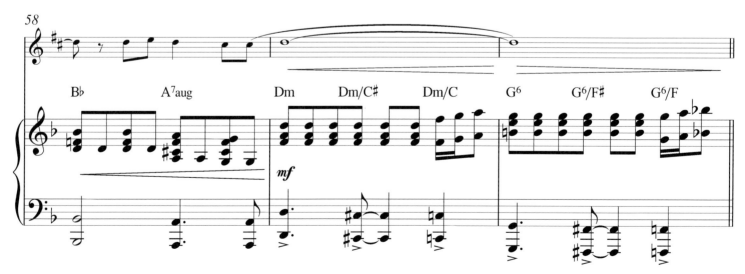

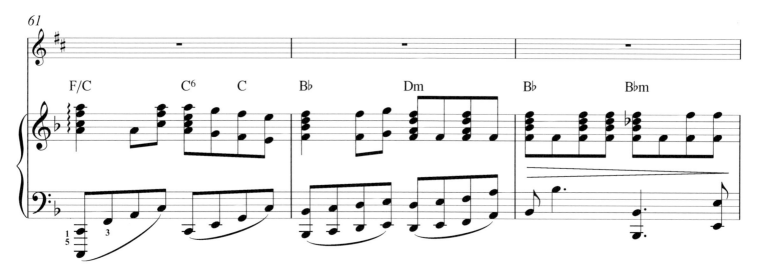

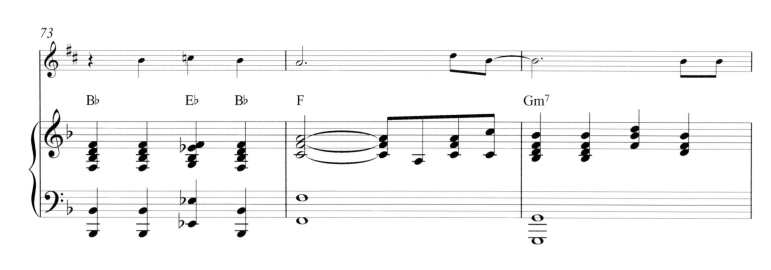

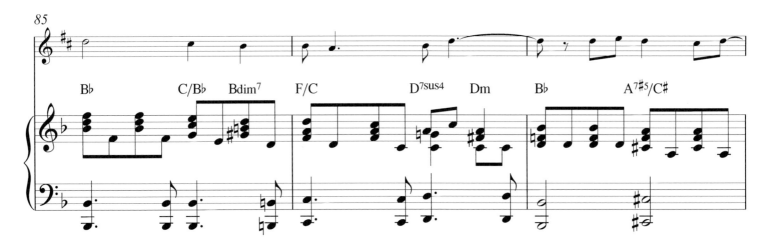

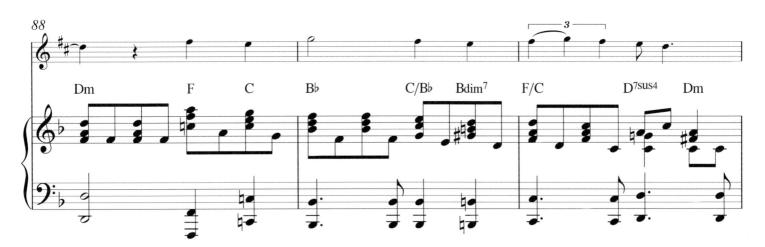

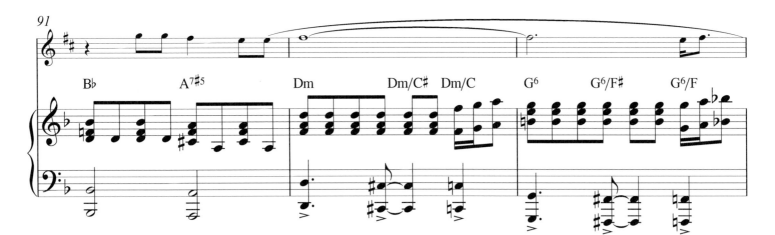

rall.

CLOCKS

Words & Music by Guy Berryman, Jonathan Buckland,
William Champion & Christopher Martin

Hints & Tips: Keep the left hand crisp and on the beat and pay attention to keeping a steady pulse. From bar 53 there is a repeated quaver pattern in the right hand played with the 5th finger — make sure the quavers are even as this finger can get tired quite quickly.

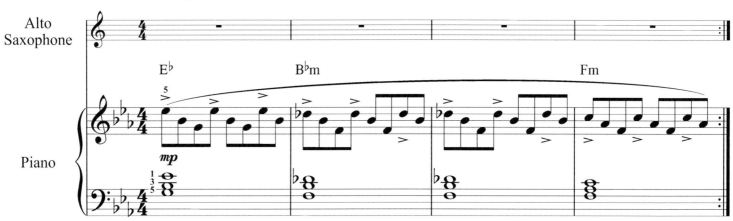

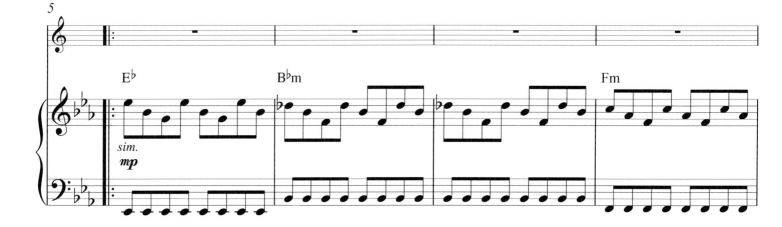

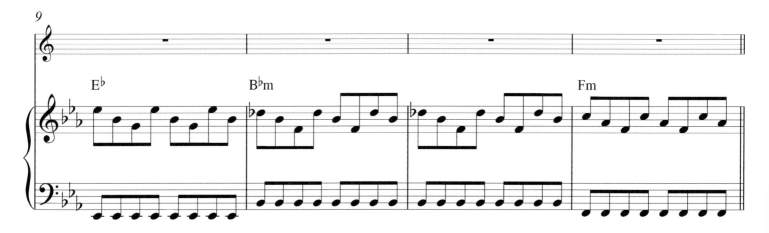

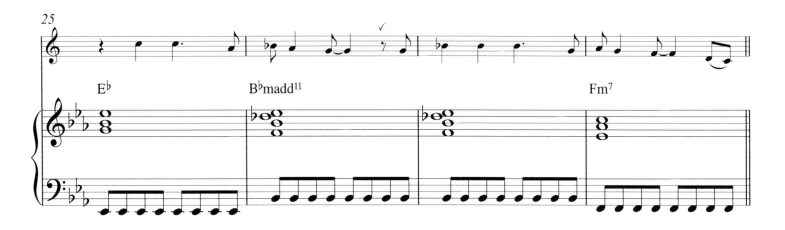

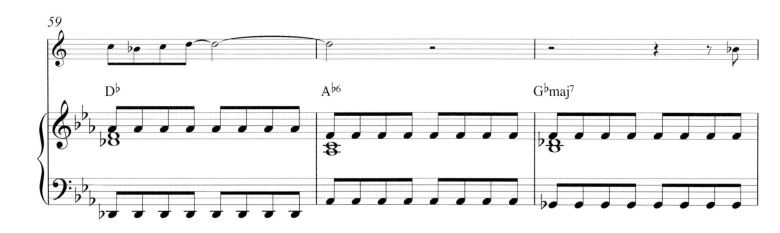

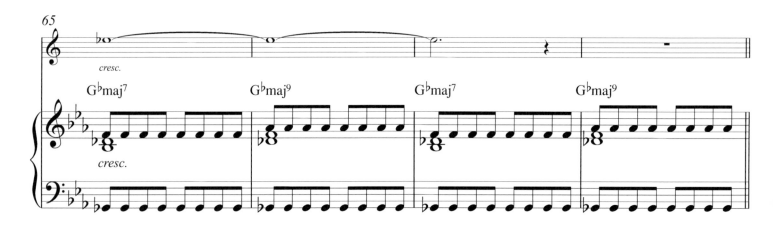

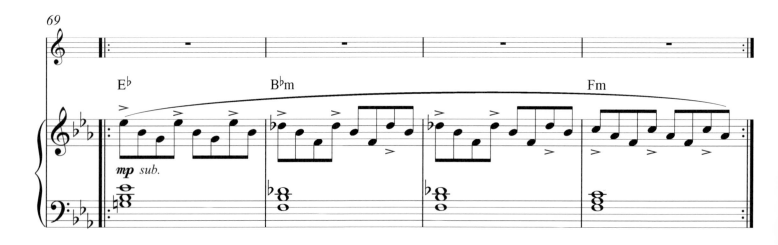

Play 4 times

DON'T STOP BELIEVIN'

Words & Music by Steve Perry, Neal Schon & Jonathan Cain

Hints & Tips: Bring out the famous bass line in the left hand and watch out for the off-beat rhythms — make sure you count carefully to ensure every note falls in the right place. Work with the soloist to ensure you play your shared rhythms exactly together in the chorus (e.g. bars 41 and 42).

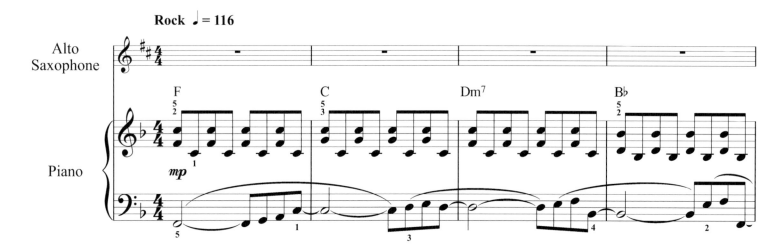

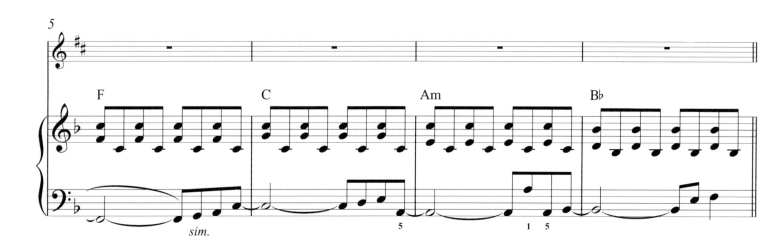

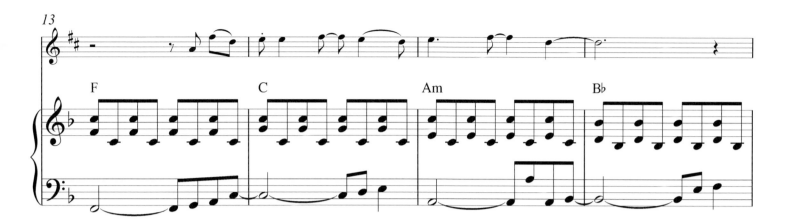

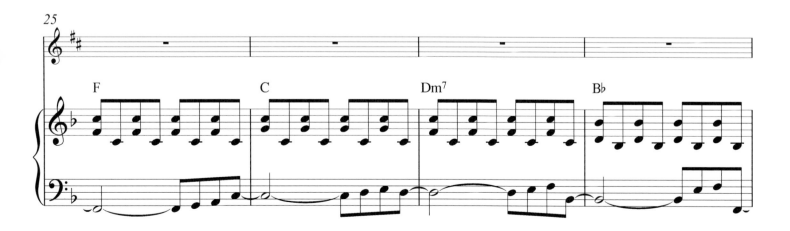

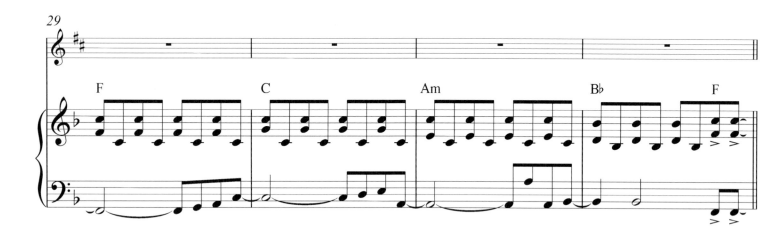

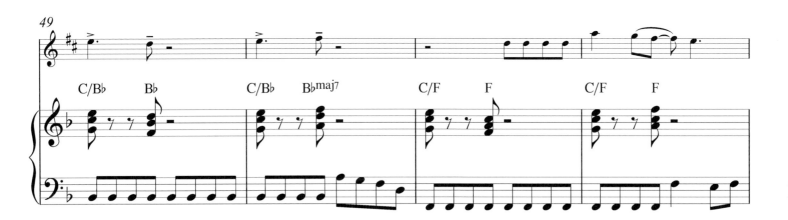

To Coda ⊕

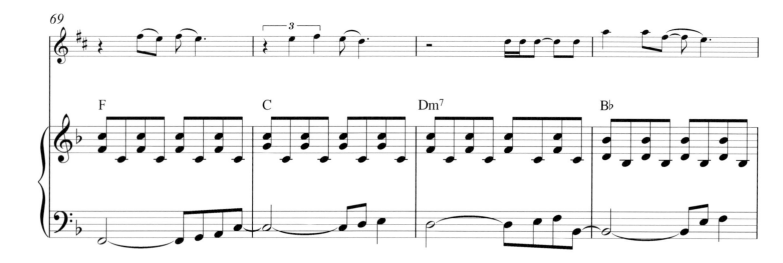

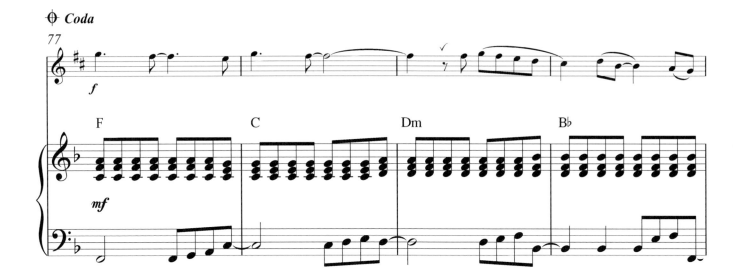

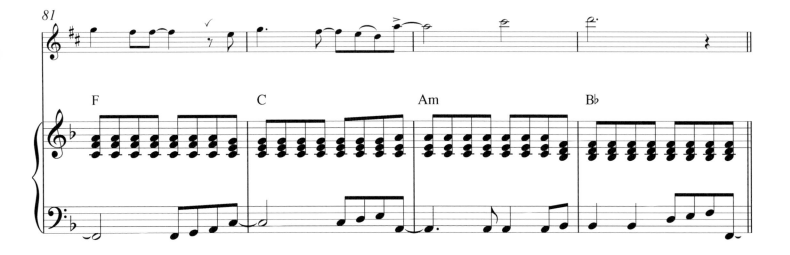

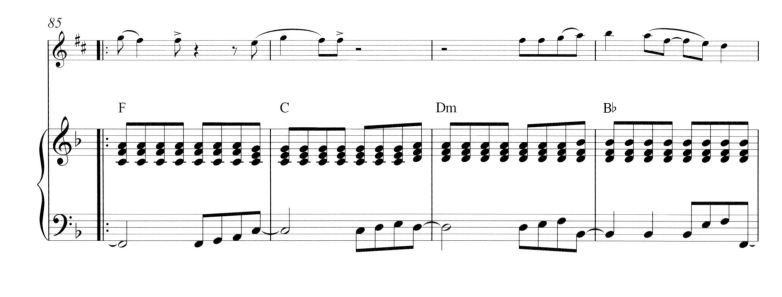

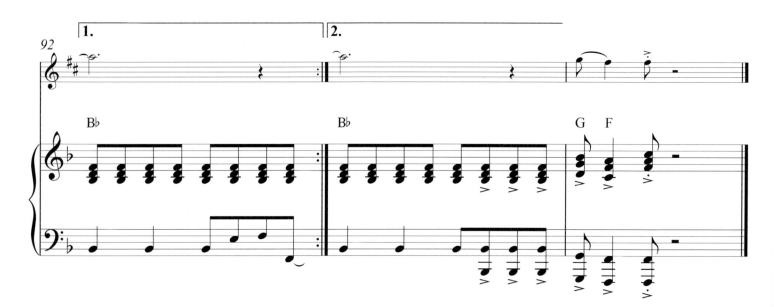

FIREWORK

Words & Music by Tor Erik Hermansen, Katy Perry,
Mikkel S. Eriksen, Sandy Wilhelm & Ester Dean

Hints & Tips: Make sure the driving quaver pattern in crisp and clear throughout.
Watch out for the change to off-beat rhythms at bar 45!

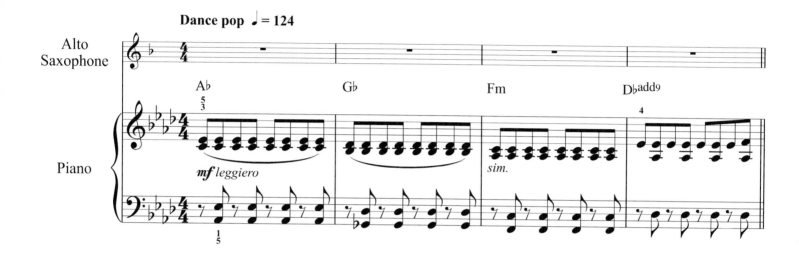

Alto Sax Part

POP PERFORMANCE PIECES

Published by
Chester Music
part of Wise Music Group
14-15 Berners Street,
London W1T 3LJ, UK.

Exclusive Distributors:
Hal Leonard
7777 West Bluemound Road,
Milwaukee, WI 53213
Email: info@halleonard.com

Hal Leonard Europe Limited
42 Wigmore Street, Marylebone,
London WIU 2 RY
Email: info@halleonardeurope.com

Hal Leonard Australia Pty. Ltd.
4 Lentara Court, Cheltenham,
Victoria 9132, Australia
Email: info@halleonard.com.au

Order No. CH85063
ISBN 978-1-78558-334-6

Piano scores are transposed.
Chord symbols at concert pitch.

Alto saxophone consultant: Howard McGill.
Piano consultant: Lisa Cox.
Compiled and edited by Naomi Cook.
Music formatted by Sarah Lofthouse, SEL Music Art Ltd.

Photographs courtesy of Ruth Keating,
assisted by Lisa Cox and James Welland.
Special thanks to the pupils at St Benedict's School, Ealing and
their Director of Music Christopher Eastwood for taking part in
the photo shoot.

Printed in the EU.

www.halleonard.com

POP PERFORMANCE PIECES

Alto Saxophone Part

CHESTER MUSIC

ALL OF ME

Words & Music by John Legend & Tobias Gad

Hints & Tips: There are lots of repeated notes in this song; try to keep them connected with gentle articulation and a warm tone. The middle eight from bar 54 is syncopated, i.e. played on the off-beats. Make sure you stay in time and don't rush!

BRIDGE OVER TROUBLED WATER

Words & Music by Paul Simon

Hints & Tips: The octave glissando from bar 15 to 16 (and 43 to 44) is a tricky one: try to run up a D major scale as quickly as possible and try to 'smear' all the notes together. This is a very useful skill on the sax. The verses are in the low register; try to play with a rich, sonorous tone.

CLOCKS

Words & Music by Guy Berryman, Jonathan Buckland,
William Champion & Christopher Martin

Hints & Tips: This number can be played with strong rhythmic intensity, giving the crotchets a good accent.
Quavers on beat one could be played staccato to emphasise the syncopation.

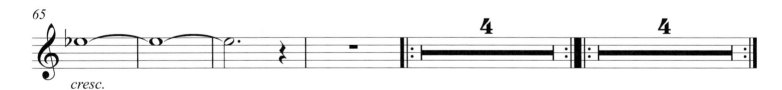

DON'T STOP BELIEVIN'

Words & Music by Steve Perry, Neal Schon & Jonathan Cain

Hints & Tips: What a great anthem to play on the alto, especially the loud and proud coda section!
Make sure you don't go sharp on the A, C# and D in bars 83 and 84.

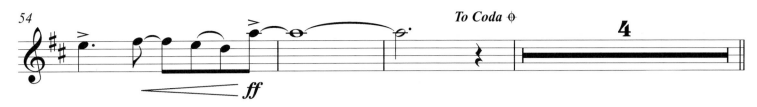

FIREWORK

Words & Music by Tor Erik Hermansen, Katy Perry,
Mikkel S. Eriksen, Sandy Wilhelm & Ester Dean

Hints & Tips: This has quite a simple, repetitive melody so it requires you to deliver it in a musical way, building to bar 13. Let the chorus sing out in the altissimo register from bar 28. Bars 46, 48, 50 and 70 are great for staccato tongue practice — make sure the tongue is placed gently on the reed making a 'T' sound.

A THOUSAND MILES

Words & Music by Vanessa Carlton

Hints & Tips: There are some challenging rhythms in this song: keep feeling the semiquaver subdivision all the way through and lock into your very own internal drum machine! Use the bis key throughout for B♭. Check your A♭ isn't sticking!

D.S. al Coda

✛ **Coda**

f

p

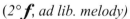
(2°**f**, ad lib. melody)

mf

1. **2.**

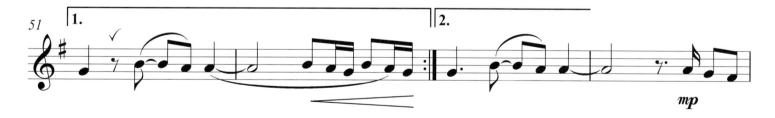

mp

p **2**

A THOUSAND YEARS

Words & Music by David Hodges & Christina Perri

Hints & Tips: This piece has a 12/8 groove, i.e. there are 4 beats in a bar with each one subdivided into a triplet. This all changes in bar 10, when you have to carefully place a 'two against three'. Try to sing this rhythm to yourself before playing the song.

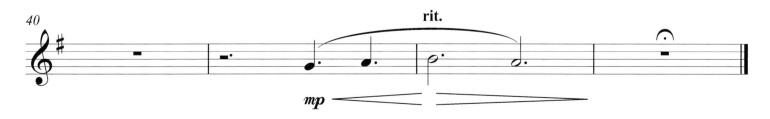

WHEN WE WERE YOUNG

Words & Music by Adele Adkins & Tobias Jesso

Hints & Tips: Make sure you connect the repeated notes at the start of this song. Play with a gentle tongue, especially in bar 7. Bars 43 and 44 are great for practising syncopated rhythms.

28

30

1.

33 **2.**

3

mp

39

42

44

46

49
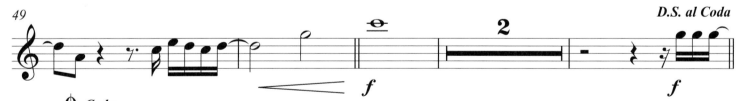

D.S. al Coda

2

f

f

⊕ **Coda**

55

mp

58

3

YOUR SONG

Words & Music by Elton John & Bernie Taupin

Hints & Tips: Try to play the opening of this song with a smooth, lyrical legato. Really make music with these phrases and try not to separate the repeated notes too much.

mf joyfully

cresc.

mp

1.

2.

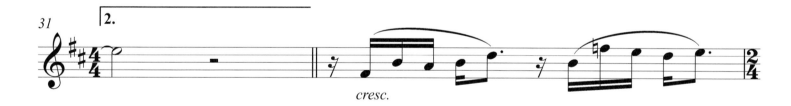

cresc.

mp

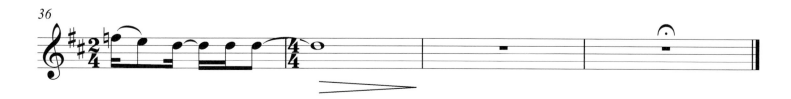

MAD WORLD

Words & Music by Roland Orzabal

Hints & Tips: This is a great song for tonguing practice as it has lots of repeated notes. It's also a good test of rhythmic placement: make sure you don't rush the syncopated notes.

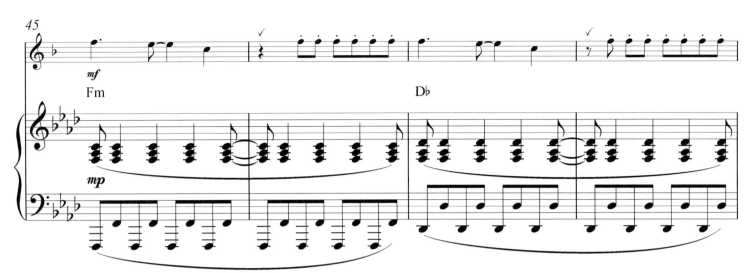

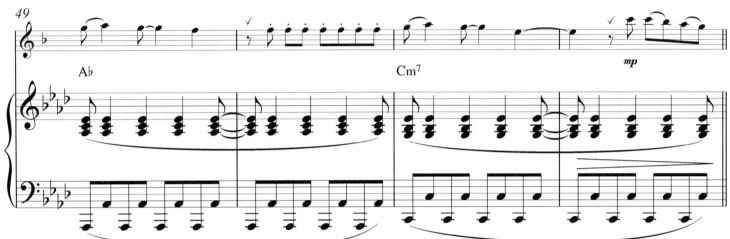

MAD WORLD

Words & Music by Roland Orzabal

Hints & Tips: Make sure the dynamic of the broken chord pattern stays the same when it switches to the right hand in bar 5. Bring out the lovely counter-melody in the right hand at bar 29. The rhythms are less predictable in the right hand from bar 22 – count carefully!

rall.

A THOUSAND YEARS

Words & Music by David Hodges & Christina Perri

Hints & Tips: There is a broad range of dynamics in this piece; make sure you make the most of these contrasts. Practise playing the right hand duplets in bar 11 against the quavers in the left hand until you are secure with the rhythms. Use the pedal to sustain the block chords in the right hand from bar 23.

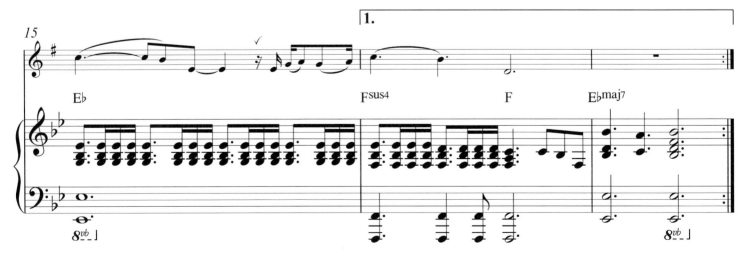

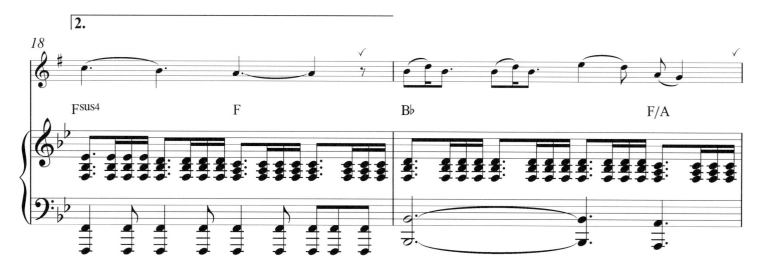

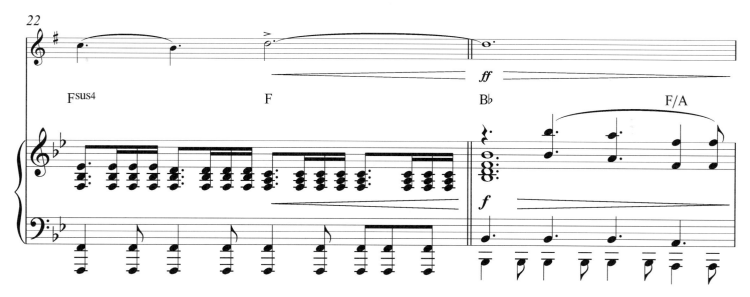

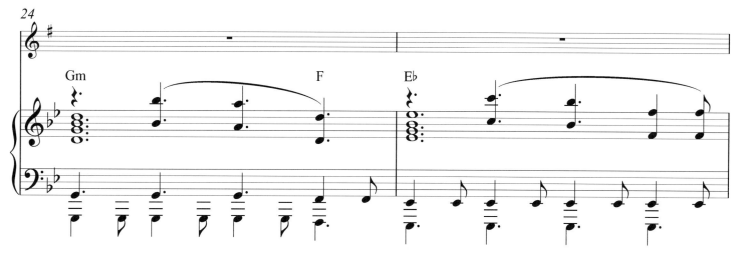

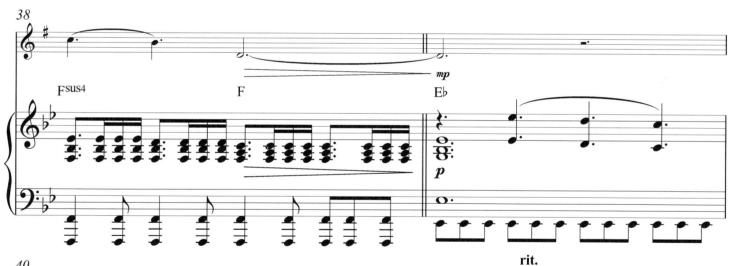

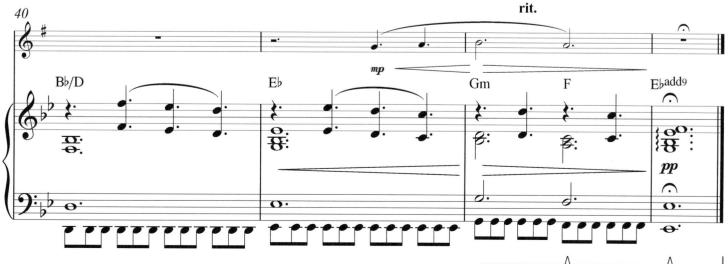

A THOUSAND MILES

Words & Music by Vanessa Carlton

Hints & Tips: This piece features a brilliant piano part! Remember to keep the semiquaver patterns crisp and even. There is a lot of movement in both hands so make sure you're ready for the octave jumps. Practise the call-and-response passages with the soloist (from bars 14 and 40), ensuring you keep to a steady tempo.

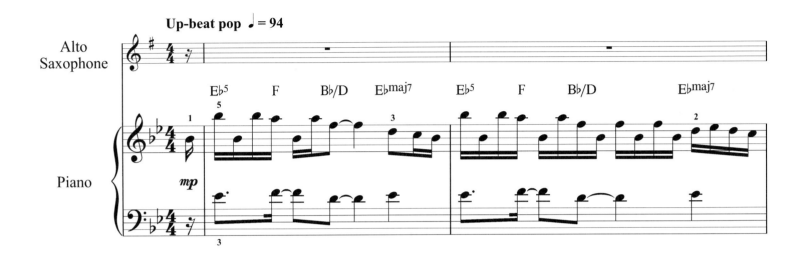

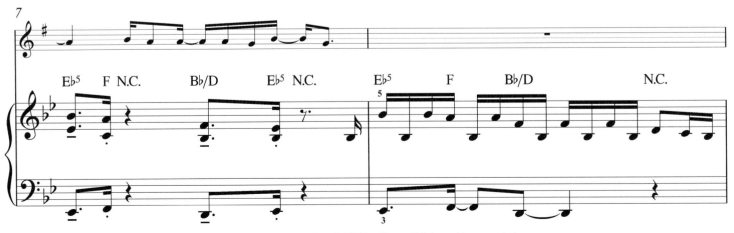

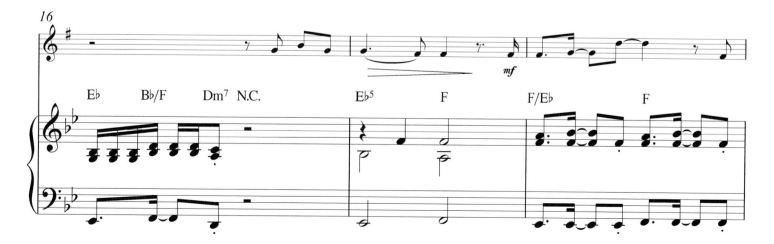

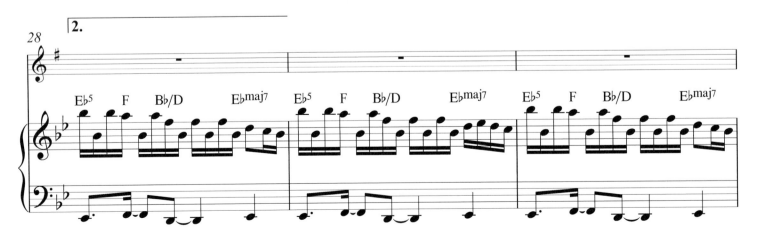

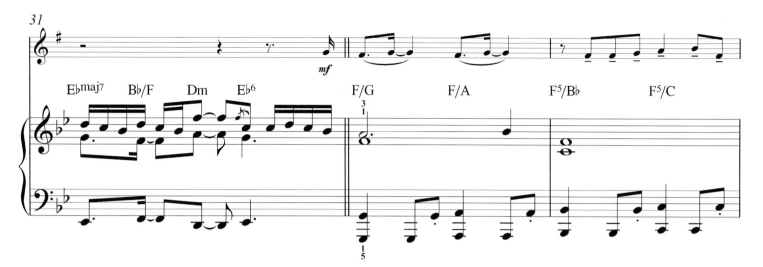

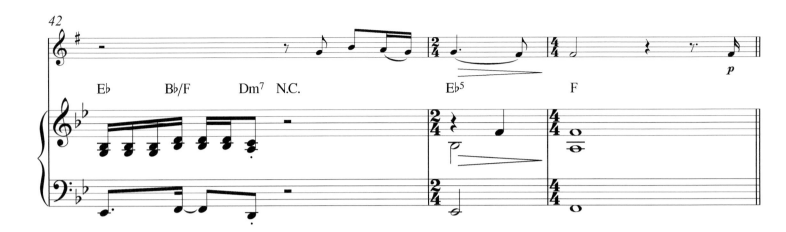

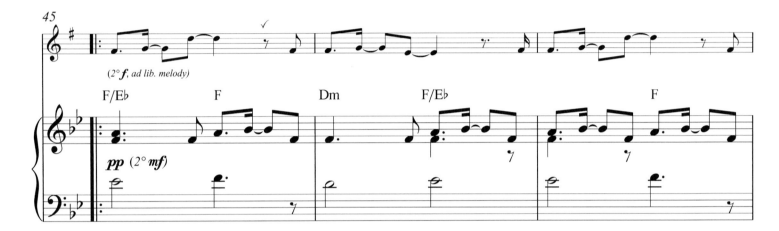

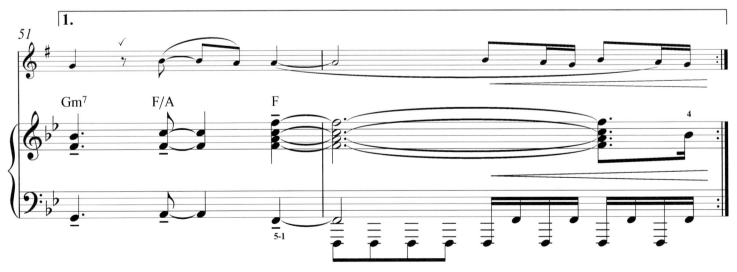

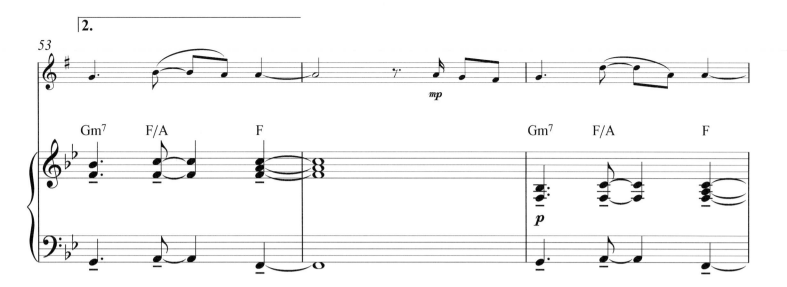

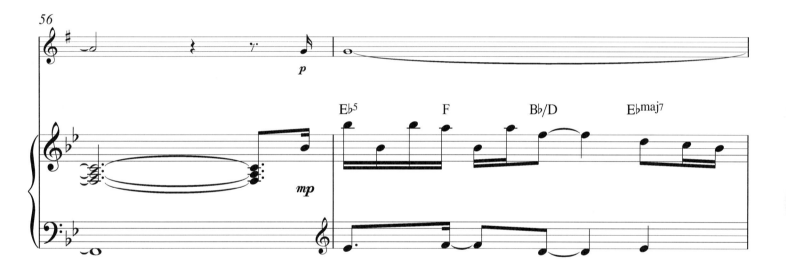

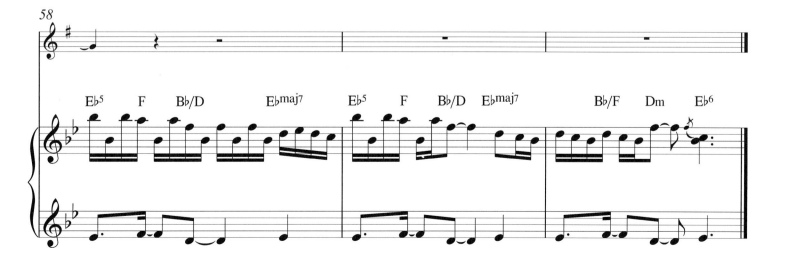

YOUR SONG

Words & Music by Elton John & Bernie Taupin

Hints & Tips: This piano part is quite busy so it's important to be sensitive to the soloist, being careful not to overpower them. Make sure you lift the pedal for every change in harmony so the sound doesn't become muddy. Some of the chords involve big stretches: play all the notes together first to get used to the shapes.

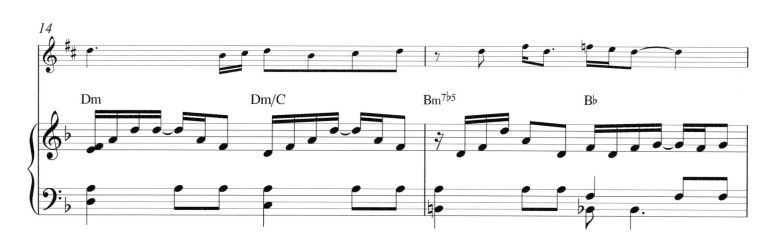

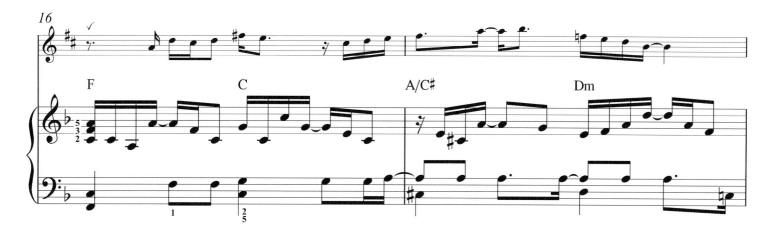

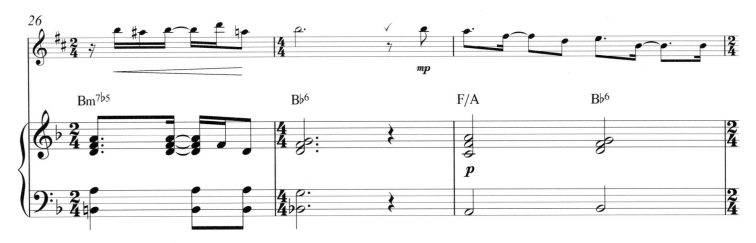

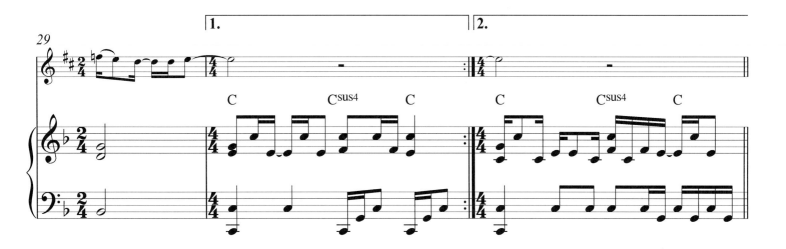

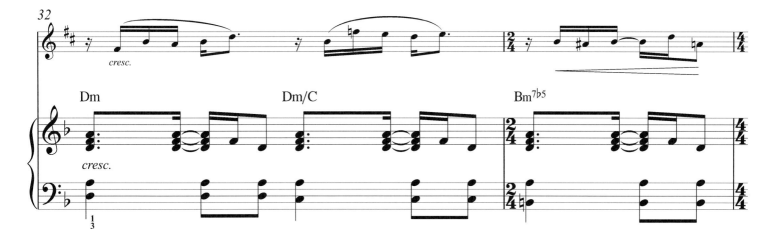

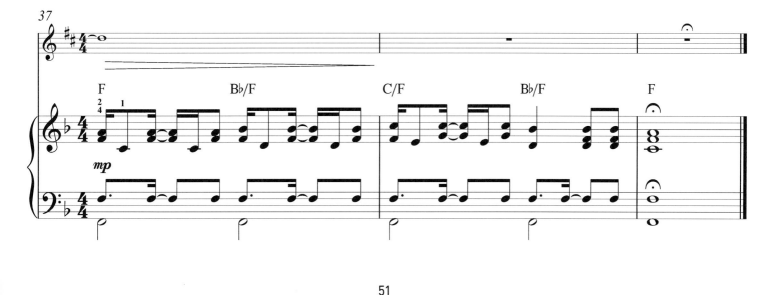

WHEN WE WERE YOUNG

Words & Music by Adele Adkins & Tobias Jesso

Hints & Tips: Work on getting the chord changes as smooth as possible and make sure you feel a steady pulse so you're not tempted to rush the held notes at the start of the piece. If the double octaves in the left hand are too big a stretch, just play the bottom note. Watch out for the big jump in both hands at bar 47!

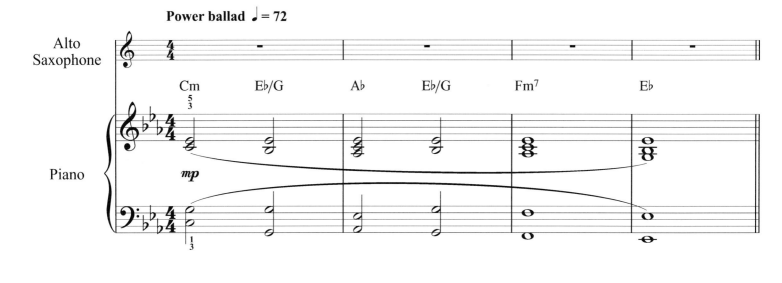

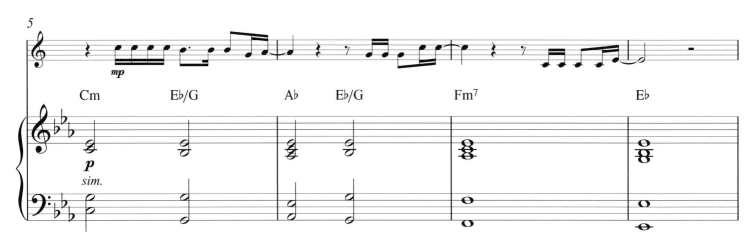

52

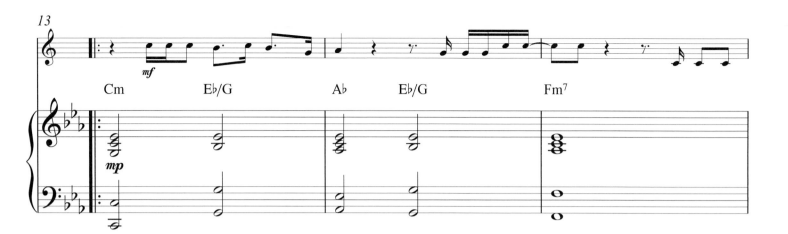

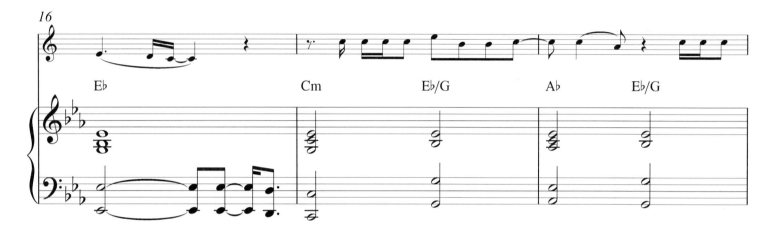

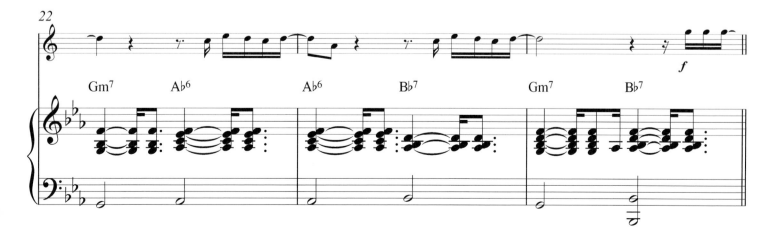

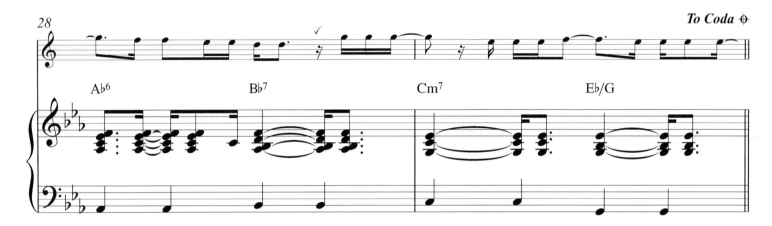

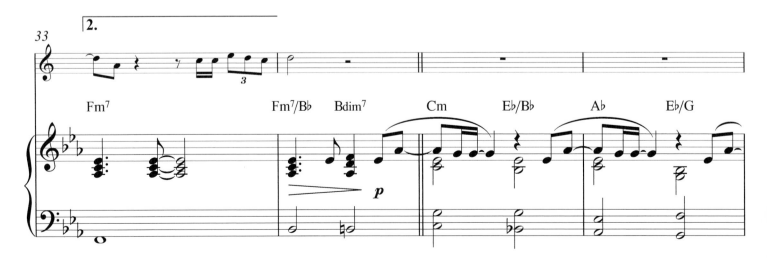

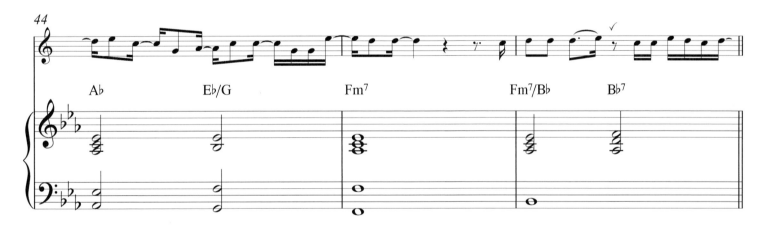

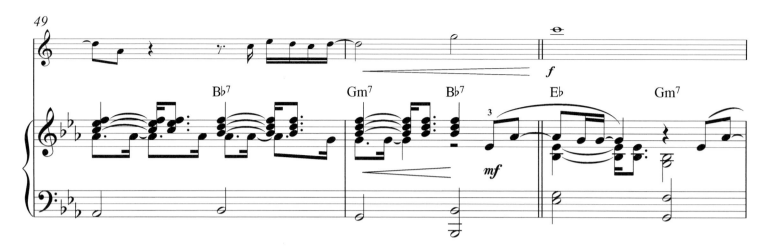

D.S. al Coda

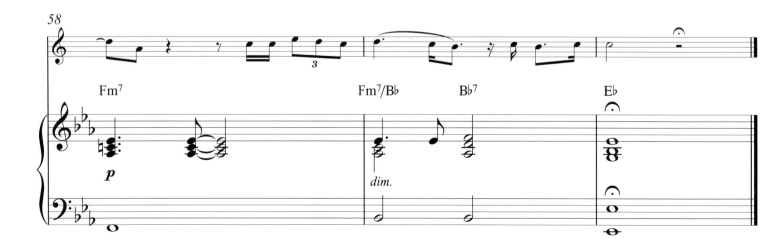